# The Philosophy Of Alfarabi
# And
# Its Influence On Medieval Thought

By
REV. ROBERT HAMMOND

THE HOBSON BOOK PRESS
52 Vanderbilt Avenue
New York 17, N. Y.
1947

Copyright 1947

By Robert Hammond

Printed in the U.S.A.

DEDICATED

TO

MY ARCHBISHOP

THE MOST REV. EDWIN V. BYRNE, D.D.

Archbishop of Santa Fe

WITH

GRATITUDE AND AFFECTION

IMPRIMATUR

†EDWIN V. BYRNE
Archbishop of Santa Fe

# PREFACE

The purpose of this book is to present, in as brief and systematic a way, the whole philosophy of Alfarabi and the influence it exerted on Medieval Thought. My efforts in this field were prompted by a sincere desire to render service to philosophy and to those who are fond of philosophy. Therefore, in outlining Alfarabi's Philosophy I shall bring out, as far as possible, the elements it has in common with Scholasticism.

My efforts will have been amply rewarded if the study of this book enables the reader to find through its pages two facts: first, that Alfarabi was well acquainted with Greek philosophy; so well acquainted, in fact, that he was able, through diligent study, to perfect some of its old theories and work out new ones. Second, that the Schoolmen borrowed from him a great amount of material which hitherto has been regarded by many as a product of their speculation, while in reality it is not. In all justice to Alfarabi and other Arabian thinkers, we should candidly admit that Christian philosophy owes a great deal to them.

It is good for the reader to know that in writing this book, I used the Arabic works of Alfarabi. I read them with care, and when anything attracted my attention, I tried to examine it closely.

My heartfelt thanks are due to my many friends for their kind encouragement and valuable suggestions. To Father Arnold Rodriguez, O. F. M., of St. Francis Cathedral, Santa Fe, I am especially indebted for his kindness in editing and typing this manuscript.

Robert Hammond

Tucumcari, New Mexico
August 10, 1946

## LIFE AND WORKS

Alfarabi, Muhammad Ben Tarkhan Abu Nasr Alfarabi, was born at Farb (now Otrar) toward the end of the ninth century of our era. Though of Turkish descent, he received his philosophical training under the tutorship of the Christian philosopher, Yuhanna Ben Hailan. Later he went to Baghdad, at that time the center of Greek philosophy. Going to Aleppo, he lived at the court of Seif-Eddaula Ali Ben Hamdan, arousing the admiration of all by his skill in dialectics. After a lengthy stay at Aleppo he went to Damascus with his patron, where he died in December of the year 950 A.D.

In logic he wrote *Introduction to Logic* and *Abridgment of Logic*. In the natural sciences he wrote commentaries on Aristotle's *Physics, Meteorology, De Coelo et Mundo*. He also wrote an essay on *The Movement of the Heavenly Spheres*.

In Psychology he wrote a commentary on Alexander of Aphrodisias' *De Anima* as well as various treatises on the *Soul*, the *Power of the Soul*, the *Unity and the One*, on the *Intelligence and the Intelligible* (i.e. on the various meanings of the word "intellect" as found in Aristotle.)

In Metaphysics he wrote essays on *Substance, Time, Space and Measure*, and various treatises entitled *The Gems of Wisdom, A Letter in Reply to Certain Questions, The Sources of Questions, The Knowledge of the Creator*.

In Ethics he wrote a commentary on the *Nicomachean Ethics of Aristotle*. Of his original works the following are best known:

*Encyclopedia*, in which he gives a brief account and definition of all branches of science and art.

*Political Regime*, which is known as the *Book of Principles*. The reading of this book is recommended by Maimonides in these terms: "I recommend you to read no works on Logic other than those of the philosopher Abu Nasr Alfarabi, since all that he wrote, especially the *Book of Principles,* is as fine flour."

# CONTENTS

PREFACE .................................................... VII
LIFE AND WORKS ...................................... IX

## INTRODUCTION

CHARACTERS OF ALFARABI'S PHILOSOPHY .... XIII
WHAT MUST PRECEDE THE STUDY OF
    PHILOSOPHY ........................................... XIV
DEFINITION AND DIVISION OF PHILOSOPHY .... XVI

## PART ONE. LOGICAL

### CHAPTER I. LOGIC

MENTAL OPERATIONS ................................. 1
CATEGORIES ................................................ 2
CERTAIN QUESTIONS ON THE CATEGORIES ...... 3

## PART TWO. THEORETICAL

### CHAPTER II. METAPHYSICS

ONTOLOGY ................................................... 10
  Universals .................................................. 10
  Description of Being ................................... 12
  Transcendental Properties of Being ............ 13
  Division of Being into Necessary and Contingent ........... 13
  Principles of Being, Potentiality and Actuality ............ 13
  The First Principles .................................... 15

METAPHYSICAL THEOLOGY ........................... 18
  Knowability of God .................................... 18
  Proofs of God's Existence ........................... 19
  Attributes of God ....................................... 22
    a)   Process of Exclusion ........................ 23
        Simplicity of God ............................ 23
        Infinity of God ............................... 25
        Immutability of God ....................... 25
        Unity of God ................................. 26

    b)   Process of pre-Eminence .................. 27
        God is Intelligent ........................... 27
        God Knows All Things through Knowledge
          of Himself .................................... 28

## CONTENTS

God is Truth ....... 28
God is Life ....... 28

### METAPHYSICAL COSMOLOGY ....... 30
Relation of God to the World ....... 30
Eternity of Matter and Eternity of the World ....... 31
Dualism of Good and Evil ....... 32

### METAPHYSICAL PSYCHOLOGY ....... 34
The Soul Is a Being Quite Distinct from the Body ....... 34
Spirituality of the Human Soul ....... 34
Immortality of the Human Soul ....... 35

## CHAPTER III. PSYCHOLOGY

A GENERAL OUTLINE OF THE POWERS OF THE SOUL ....... 37
1. Powers of Knowledge ....... 38
   Sense-Knowledge ....... 38
   Perceptive Knowledge ....... 40
   Abstractive Knowledge ....... 41

2. Powers of Action ....... 45
   Sensitive Appetite ....... 45
   Intellective Appetite ....... 46

## PART THREE. PRACTICAL

## CHAPTER IV. ETHICS

ACTIONS GOOD, BAD, OR INDIFFERENT ....... 49

## CHAPTER V. POLITICAL SOCIETY

DESCRIPTION OF THE MODEL STATE ....... 50

## CONCLUDING CHAPTER

THREE CONCLUSIONS ....... 54

BIBLIOGRAPHY ....... 57
INDEX ....... 59

# INTRODUCTION

## CHARACTERS OF ALFARABI'S PHILOSOPHY

Alfarabi is a Neo-Platonist inasmuch as his mystic tendencies are numerous in his Metaphysics, Psychology and Political thought. As a Neo-Platonist, he follows the groundwork of the Neo-Platonic doctrine made of religious Mysticism and Emanatist Monism. Thus, Alfarabi's philosophy is entirely theocentric in the sense that it holds God as the center of the universe. God is One; this One is the Absolute which transcends everything. From the One flows the plurality of things gradually coming down the scale of perfection to the existence of matter. The goal of man is to return to God. This return is to be accomplished by virtue and philosophical thought.

Like the Neo-Platonists, Alfarabi holds in his treatise on *The Agreement Between Plato and Aristotle,* that there is no essential difference between the philosophy of Plato and that of Aristotle.[1] Therefore, the Emanatist Monism as well as the reconciliation of Plato and Aristotle may be regarded as the outstanding features which make Alfarabi's philosophy depend on

---

[1] Alfarabi, *On The Agreement Between Plato and Aristotle,* in Collection of various treatises. Arabic ed. Cairo 1907. Muhammad Ismail, pp. 1-39.

The main theories of Plato and Aristotle that need to be reconciled are the following:

a) Some thought that a world of difference existed between Plato and Aristotle, because Plato, in his *Timaeus,* says that the noblest substance is the nearest to the soul and intellect, and therefore the farthest from the senses. Aristotle, on the other hand, says that the noblest substance is the individual (first substance). Here the disagreement between Plato and Aristotle, in Alfarabi's mind, is not real, because both of them speak of the same thing from a different point of view. For Aristotle the individual is nobler in Logic, because in Logic he sees beings lying in the region of the senses, and from them he abstracts the universal, the rational, the intelligible. For Plato the universal is nobler in Metaphysics, because there he sees beings that cannot change and will not change. [op. cit. pp. 8-10]

b) With regard to the theory of knowledge, Alfarabi interpreted the Platonic hypothesis of reminiscence in an empiric sense. He says

*(Continued on next page)*

# INTRODUCTION

that of Plotinus. But outside of these Neo-Platonic features, all the philosophy of Alfarabi may be said to be saturated with Aristotelism which, by its empirical method, suited better his scientific mind.

## WHAT MUST PRECEDE THE STUDY OF PHILOSOPHY

Alfarabi lays down several rules for teachers honestly striving to train youth in philosophy. No youth should start the study of philosophy before he is well acquainted with the natural sciences. For, human nature requires a gradual rise from the imperfect to the perfect. Mathematics is a very important subject in training the mind of the young philosopher because it helps him pass easily from the sensible to the intelligible, and also because it familiarizes his mind with exact demonstrations.[2]

The study of Logic, as an instrument to distinguish the true from the false, is of great educational value before beginning the study of philosophy proper.[3]

(*Continued from preceding page*)
that Aristotle proved in Analytics that our ideas are acquired by means of the senses, and because of that, they are by no means a reminiscence. Their formation, however, occurs so rapidly and unconsciously that the soul comes to imagine it has had them all the time, so that thinking of them would seem to the soul like recollecting or remembering them. According to Alfarabi, Plato held the same opinion when he said that to think is to recollect, for the person who thinks tries to get at what experience has written on his mind, and once he finds the object of his thought, then it looks to him as if he had recollected. [op. cit. pp 23-25]

c) Alfarabi does not agree with the opinion of his contemporaries, who hold that Aristotle believed in the existence of the world *ab aeterno*, while Plato did not. According to him, the true teaching of Aristotle was that time is the measurement of the motion of the world, and consequently, the product of motion. That explains why he was obliged to believe that God created the world without time, and that time is the result of the motion of the world. [op. cit. pp. 26-27]

[2]Alfarabi, *What Must Precede the Study of Philosophy*, in Collection of various treatises, 1 Arabic ed., Cairo, 1907, Muhammad Ismail, n. 3, p. 61.

[3]Id. op. cit. n. 3, p. 62.

## INTRODUCTION

The training of one's own character, instincts and tendencies must come before entering into philosophy, for unless that is done, the chances are that the student will never fully grasp the higher and more solid truths, because his mind is still clouded by sensibility.[4]

Philosophy is studied primarily to obtain a knowledge of God as the Creator and Efficient Cause of all things, the One, Immovable.[5]

The student of philosophy must be instructed in the sources from which the different philosophies take their names. For example, he should be told that some philosophies derive their names from the manner in which they are taught, such as the philosophy of Peripateticism, which was discussed with students while walking up and down a garden. He should be taught that other philosophies take their names from the author, such as Platonism from Plato and Aristotelism from Aristotle; and that others take their names from the goal they propose, such as Epicurism, setting pleasure as an end.[6]

In teaching, two extremes must be avoided. The teacher must be neither excessively strict nor excessively lenient. For, if he is too strict he errs through excess and if he is too lenient, he errs through defect. If the teacher becomes unpopular because of his severity, his excessive leniency will also tend to make him unworthy of respect. The teacher, therefore, should avoid excess as well as defect.[7]

The young man must be persuaded to persevere in the study of philosophy by calling his attention now and then to the old Arabic saying, "The drop wears away the stone", — "Gutta cavat lapidem".[8]

The teacher should see that his student attends only to one

[4]Id. op. cit. n. 3, p. 62
[5]Id. op. cit. n. 4, p. 62
[6]Id. op. cit. n. 1, p. 58
[7]Id. op. cit. n. 8, p. 63
[8]Id. op. cit. n. 8, p. 63

## INTRODUCTION

thing at a time. For, only one thing can be well mastered at a time. The reason for this rule is to have the student concentrate his attention upon the object of study and make a success of it.[9]

## DEFINITION AND DIVISION OF PHILOSOPHY

For Alfarabi, philosophy is nothing else than thought, that is, the science of concepts. The end of philosophy is to know God as the Creator of heaven and earth.

Alfarabi's philosophy can be divided into Logic, Theoretical philosophy and Practical philosophy. The Theoretical could be subdivided into Metaphysics and Psychology, while the Practical philosophy into Ethics and Politics.

I  LOGIC

II  THEORETICAL  —Metaphysics
                                —Psychology

III  PRACTICAL  —Ethics
                             —Politics

[9] Id. op. cit. n. 8, p. 63

# PART I
# LOGICAL

## Chapter I
## LOGIC

In Logic Alfarabi follows Aristotle. He has, however, his own original views. His Logic deals with concepts, judgments and reasoning.

### MENTAL OPERATIONS

According to Alfarabi, a concept is an idea that represents the objective essence or the essential notes of a thing. It is the object of the first mental operation, called conception. "Concepts," says Alfarabi, "are determined by definition; definition declares what a thing is. Through definition concepts are so arranged and systematized that they imply one another until we arrive at the most universal ones, which do not presuppose others, such as Being, Necessary Being, Contingent Being. Such concepts are self-evident. A man's mind may be directed to them and his soul may be cognizant of them, but they cannot be demonstrated to him. Nor can they be explained by deriving them from what is known, since they are already clear in themselves, and that with the highest degree of ceritude."[10]

For Alfarabi, judgment is the combination of a particular entity with a universal idea. The synthesis of the particular with the universal is never evident of itself. That explains why we must seek a second universal with which the first universal and the particular agree. Once we find a second universal with which the two terms of the judgment agree, both of these will agree too, between themselves, according to the principle which is the supreme law of every syllogism, "Two things which are equal to the same thing, are equal to each other." Thus, for instance, the judgment, "The world is made" is not so clear as to permit the union of the particular "world" with the universal "made". There is a term of mediation for both, and this is the universal "Composed".[11]

[10] Alfarabi, *The Sources of Questions*, in Collection, op. cit. n. 1, p. 65.
[11] Alfarabi, *The Sources of Questions*, in Collection, op. cit. n. 2, p. 65.

In Alfarabi's opinion, the process of reasoning by which we start from what is known and well established and proceed to a knowledge of the unknown, is Logic strictly speaking.[12] Philosophy, therefore, is mediation, reasoning and demonstration. Is philosophy only that and nothing else? Certainly not. There is something that cannot be mediated or demonstrated, namely, the First Principles.

The First Principles are those of Contradiction, Causality and of Excluded Middle. Such principles are self-evident, because they have in themselves their own demonstration.

## THE CATEGORIES

All our concepts could be classified under ten headings, called categories. For, the categories are a complete enumeration of everything that can enter into judgment, either as a subject or predicate. Alfarabi, following Aristotle, enumerates ten: Substance, Quantity, Quality, Relation, Place, Time, Action, Passion, Posture and Having. Such categories, in Alfarabi's view, have been empirically gathered by Aristotle. Observing the things which make the universe, Aristotle found that some of them exist in themselves and are basis of certain accidents or differences. The things existing in themselves he called "substances" and the differences he called "accidents."

Aristotle then asked, "How many kinds of accidents are there?" He noticed that substance is divisible and therefore capable of more or less; thus he named Quantity the first accident-category. Realizing that substance has capacity of acquiring certain characteristics, like, "Peter is good," Paul is a philosopher," Aristotle lost no time in selecting Quality as the second accident-category.

Because substances are inter-related in the sense that the concept of one implies the other, Aristotle lost no time in choosing

[12]Id. op. cit. n. 2, p. 66.

# THE PHILOSOPHY OF ALFARABI 3

Relation as the third accident-category. The relation between time and a thing in time led him to name Time in the fourth place. Because of the relation between different objects in space or the relation between place and the thing placed, Aristotle set aside Place as the fifth accident-category. The ability of substance to take various positions helped him select Posture as the sixth accident-category. The physical influence of substance on the production of another substance made him call Action as the seventh accident-category. Since substance is influenced by the efficient cause, he chose Passion as the eighth accident-category. Finally the relation of the thing having and the thing had made him pick Having as the ninth accident-category.[13]

## CERTAIN QUESTIONS ON THE CATEGORIES

In treating the Categories, Alfarabi gave the answer to certain questions that had worried the Logicians of his time. First of all, he believes that not all the ten Categories are absolutely simple. Each is simple when compared with those that are below it. But only four are absolutely simple, namely, Substance, Quality, Quantity and Posture. Action and Passion come from substance and quality; time and place from substance and quantity; Having occurs between two substances; Relation between two of the ten categories.[14]

There are degrees in the simplicity of the Categories. For instance, Quantity and Quality depend directly on substance, so much so that to exist both need only a substance. On the contrary, Relation needs several things, perhaps two substances, or a substance and an accident, or two accidents.[15]

When asked whether Action and Passion, which are found together, should be classified in the category of Relation, Alfarabi

---

[13] Alfarabi, *A Letter in Reply to Certain Questions*, in Collection, op. cit. n. 25, pp. 103-105.
[14] Alfarabi, *A Letter in Reply to Certain Questions*, in Collection, op. cit. n. 19, pp. 98-99.
[15] Id. op. cit. n. 13, p. 98.

answers in the negative. For "when we find one thing always with another," he says, "it does not follow that there is a dependence of relation between them." For example, we find respiration only with the lungs, the day only with sunrise, accident only with substance, the spoken word only with the tongue. Now all these things are not to be classified in the dependence of Relation, but rather in that of necessity. Necessity may be essential necessity, as that of the birth of the day upon the rising of the sun; and accidental necessity as that of the departure of Zeid upon the arrival of Amron. Furthermore, there is complete necessity when one thing exists by reason of the other, as father and son; while it is incomplete necessity when the dependence of relation is unilateral, as one and two, the two depends on the one, but the one does not depend on the two.[16]

We ask whether the Equal and the Unequal are a property of Quantity, and the Similar and Dissimilar a property of Quality. According to Alfarabi, each of the two terms Equal and Unequal, taken separately, is a property of Quantity, while if both terms are taken together, they are descriptive of Quantity. The same is true of Similar and Dissimilar in reference to Quality.[17]

In regard to the theory of Contraries, Alfarabi makes some very profound observations. "Is the contrary the absence (privation) of its contrary? Is white the absence of black?" asks Alfarabi. He answers saying, "It is not. For, white is something and not merely the absence of black. Since the absence of black is a fact in the existence of white, we are led to say that every contrary is the absence of its contrary."[18]

People say that the science of the contraries is one. But Alfarabi says that a distinction must be made, for "If we deal with the science of something which happens to have a contrary, then that science is not identical with that of its contrary. The

[16]Id. op. cit. n. 18, p. 98.
[17]Id. op. cit. n. 24, p. 102.
[18]Id. op. cit. n. 17, pp. 97-98.

science of the Just is not that of the Unjust, the knowledge of White is not the knowledge of Black. On the other hand, if we deal with the science of something insofar as it has a contrary, then this science is one with that of its contrary, because in this sense the two contraries are really and truly two relatives."[19]

"Opposites and Contraries differ and must be distinguished one from the other," says Alfarabi. "Opposites are two things which cannot exist in the same object at the same time and in the same respect, as the quality of father and son. Opposites are a part of Relatives proper. Contraries are odd and even, affirmation and negation, sight and blindness."[20]

Some ask how many things are necessary to the knowledge of the unknown. "Two things are necessary and sufficient," answers Alfarabi. "If there are more than two, this means that they are not necessary to the knowledge of the object under investigation."[21]

"Is the proposition, "Man exists" a judgment with or without a predicate?" asks Alfarabi. "If man is considered from the natural and objective viewpoint," he answers, "the judgment is without a predicate because the fact of existence is one with man and cannot be distinguished from him, while the predicate denotes distinction from the thing to which it is referred. From a logical point of view, the judgment has a predicate, because it is made up of two terms which may be either true or false."[22]

In Logic too Alfarabi makes some brilliant and original observations, and gives evidence of a great knowledge of the Organon and Isagoge.

---

[19]Id. op. cit. n. 37, p. 109.
[20]Id. op. cit. n. 38, pp. 109-110.
[21]Id. op. cit. n. 29, pp. 106-107.
[22]Id. op. cit. n. 16, p. 97.

# THEORETICAL PHILOSOPHY

## PART II

## Chapter II

## METAPHYSICS

## MEANING AND DIVISION

"Particular sciences," says Alfarabi, "restrict themselves to one or several departments of being. For instance, physics is the science of being as affected by physical properties. Mathematics is the science of being which deals with quantities and numbers. Medicine is the science of being insofar as it is healthy or sick. Metaphysics, however, knows no such restrictions. Its field is all reality, namely, Being. And it is all equally extensive with the concept of Being (One, True, Good.)"[23]

Metaphysics, in the opinion of Alfarabi, treats of things which are separate from matter. In this connection he distinguishes two kinds of immaterial: the first, *immaterial quoad esse* or immaterial beings, such as God and the human soul, which exist without matter; and the second, *immaterial quoad conceptum,* or concepts, such as substance, accident, cause, quality, the content of which is free from all matter.

Metaphysics, insofar as it treats of immaterial concepts, of those general notions in which matter is not included, may be called General Metaphysics or Ontology, that is, the science of Being. And because it treats of immaterial beings, it may be called Special Metaphysics. It could then be divided into three parts: Metaphysical Theology, which deals with God and His attributes; Metaphysical Cosmology, which treats of the ultimate principles of the universe; and finally Metaphysical Psychology, which treats of the human soul.

Since Alfarabi holds that immaterial may be *quoad esse* and *quoad conceptum,* his whole metaphysical thought may be divided accordingly, that is, into Ontology, Metaphysical Theology, Metaphysical Cosmology and Metaphysical Psychology.

[23] Alfarabi, *The Scope of Aristotle In The Book of Metaphysics*, in Collection, op. cit. pp. 40-44.

## -1-

## ONTOLOGY

### UNIVERSALS

The mind, in all its operations, exerts the function of synthesizing the many in the one. In fact, we cannot understand the meaning of a scene presented to our senses unless we unite its parts into a perceived whole. Perception is an act of the mind which involves synthesizing. The act of imagination involves both analysis and synthesis in the sense that nothing can be imagined without synthesizing the many in the one. The act of judgment, whereby one thing is affirmed or denied of another, cannot be had except by synthesizing both terms, subject and predicate, in one act of comparison. Syllogism, too, is simply the synthesis of two judgments in a third one. Of all these operations of the mind, the concept, more than all others, represents the synthesizing function of the mind, for the concept is by definition the apprehension of the one in the many.

For Alfarabi the concept means exactly that and nothing more. "The concept," he says, "has a content signifying the synthetic, the universal, the one. The universal in reference to the particular is like the genus and species in reference to individuals. The individuals, called "First Substances," precede the universal, called "Second Substances." The former alone have substantial existence, and because of that, one is led to think that First Substances are more substances than the Second Substances. On the other hand, the universal, being permanent and subsistent, has more right to the name of substance than mortal individuals."[24]

"How do universals exist?" asks Alfarabi. "The universals

[24]Alfarabi, *A Letter in Reply to Certain Questions*, in Collection, op. cit. n. 14, pp. 95-96.

do not exist in act," he says, "that is, they are not things existing in themselves, but they exist only in individuals, and their existence is accidental in the sense that they are subject to the existence of individuals. That does not mean, however, that universals are accidents, but merely that their existence in act can take place only per accident."

As to the definition of universals, Alfarabi says that "The universal is *unum de multis et in multis* (the one found in many and affirmed of many). The inference is that the universal has no existence apart from the individual (non habet esse separatum a multis)."[25] Here we must recall that Albertus Magnus quotes the Alfarabian definition of the universal, a fact which proves beyond all doubt that both he and his pupil, St. Thomas, were acquainted with the writings of our philosopher. [See Albertus Magnus, De praed. II, 5]

Some may ask, "Is the opinion of Alfarabi on the nature of universals right or wrong?" I hold that it is right, because he believes that the universal exists really in the individuals, and not in the manner in which it is abstracted from individual characteristics. All Christian philosophers in the Middle Ages maintained the same solution on the question of the universals. In fact, St. Thomas writes: "Universalia non habent esse in rerum natura ut sint universalia, sed solum secundum quod sunt individuata." (*De Anima,* art. 1.) In another place he says: "Universalia non sunt res subsistentes, sed habent esse solum in singularibus." (*Contra Gentiles,* Lib. I, cap LXV).

I do not agree with Munk who thinks that all Arabian philosophers are Nominalists concerning the question of universals. Alfarabi, for example, is not a Nominalist, because he holds unequivocally that the universal is blended with the individual. That some Arabian thinkers, such as Moses Maimonides, are Nominalists, I admit: but that they all are so, I cannot grant. [See Munk, *Melanges de philosophie juive et arabe,* Paris, 1859, A. Franck, p. 327]

[25]Id. op. cit. N. 10, p. 94.

## DESCRIPTION OF BEING

"The most universal concept," says Alfarabi, "is Being and what is coextensive with Being itself (One, True, Good)." "Being cannot be defined," he says, "for it is self-evident, fixed in the mind, precedes all other concepts and is the simplest of all. It is the simplest, because to define a concept is to analyze its content, and Being, having the least content, resists all efforts to resolve it into simpler thought elements. To try to define it by words serves only to make our mind attentive and directed to it, and not to explain the concept which is clearer than the words by which it is defined." He goes on to say that "Just as in the demonstration of a proposition it is imperative that the judgments be coordinated in order to arrive at an ultimate judgment-principle, in like manner in the definition of a concept, it is necessary that the concept be resolved into other simpler concepts until one arrives at the simplest and most universal concept, which is Being."[26] Now, St. Thomas describes Being in much the same way. Not only does he unfold the same ideas as those of Alfarabi, but the suprising thing is that the ideas are couched in exactly the same words as those of Alfarabi. A glance at the writings of both Alfarabi and St. Thomas bears this out.

Here is what St. Thomas says about Being:

> Illud autem quod primo intellectus concipit quasi notissimum, et in quo omnes conceptiones resolvit, est ens.[27]

In another place he says:

> Videlicet, ens, unum, verum, bonum; quae re idem sunt, sed ratione distinguuntur. Sicut enim in demonstrationibus resolvere oportet omnes propositiones usque ad principia ipsa, ad quae necesse est stare rationem, ita in apprehensione praedictorum oportet stare ad ens quod in quolibet cognito naturaliter cognoscitur, sicut et principium in omnibus propositionibus que sunt post principia.[28]

[26] Alfarabi, *The Sources of Questions*, in Collection, op. cit., n. 1-2, p. 65.
[27] St. Thomas, Quest. disp., *De Veritate*, Q. I, a. 1.
[28] St. Thomas, Opusculum XXXIX, *De Natura Generis*, cap. II.

# THE PHILOSOPHY OF ALFARABI

## TRANSCENDENTAL PROPERTIES OF BEING

For Alfarabi ens, unum, verum et bonum convertuntur. By that he means that the concept of Being coincides with that of unity, truth and goodness, and that every being is one, true and good.[29]

## DIVISION OF BEING INTO NECESSARY AND CONTINGENT

According to Alfarabi, *Necessary Being* is that which exists in itself or that which cannot but exist. *Contingent Being* is that which receives its being from another, and whose non-existence is possible.[30]

## METAPHYSICAL PRINCIPLES OF BEING POTENTIALITY AND ACTUALITY

*Potentiality* is the capability to exist. Every created being, before it existed, had only a possibility to exist: it was in potentiality. *Actuality* is that which exists in reality. That which is *in act* is perfect, and that which is in *potentiality* is imperfect. Potentiality and actuality constitute the nature of reality, which means that reality is being in becoming. This theory of potentiality and actuality is the central point in Metaphysics, toward which substance and accident, essence and existence, matter and form converge, and upon which their own value depends.

A thing, though actual at any given moment, is in potentiality in respect to future modifications. Hence, *substance* and *accident*. *Substance* is that which exists in itself and is the foundation of certain accidents or accidental differences. Its fundamental characteristic is to exist in itself and not in another as its subject.[31] *Accident* is that which needs a subject in which

---

[29] Alfarabi, *The Scope of Aristotle in the Book of Metaphysics*, in Collection, op. cit. p. 42.
[30] Alfarabi, *The Sources of Questions*, in Collection, op. cit. n. 3 p. 66.
[31] Alfarabi, *The Gems of Wisdom*, in Collection, op. cit. p. 174.

and by which it may exist. For example, a coat is a substance, because it exists in itself; white or black are accidents, because they do not exist without a substance in which they may inhere.[32]

In every created being there are two constituent principles, *essence* and *existence,* which are conceived as actuality and potentiality respectively. *Essence* is the reason why a thing is what it is. *Existence* is the actuality of essence.[33]

To the question, "What is the nature of the distinction between essence and existence in created substances?" Alfarabi replies that "A real distinction occurs here and that existence is one thing and essence is another. If essence and existence were one thing, then we should be unable to conceive the one without conceiving the other. But, in fact, we are able to conceive essence in itself. If it is true that man has existence by essence, this would be like saying that to conceive man's essence is to imply his existence." He continues with the same idea saying that "If existence should enter into composition with the essence of man like one entering into the essence of two, this would mean that it is impossible to conceive perfectly the essence of man without his existence as a part of the essence. Just as the essence of two would be destroyed by taking away a unity from it, so would the essence of man be destroyed by taking away existence from it. But this is not true, because existence does not enter into composition with the essence of a thing, for it is possible to understand the essence of man, and not to know whether it exists in reality. On the other hand, if there was no distinction between essence and existence in created beings, then these could be said to exist by their essence. But there is one being alone whose essence is His very existence, and that is God.[34]

[32]Alfarabi, *A Letter in Reply to Certain Questions*, in Collection, op. cit. n. 22, p. 101.

[33]Alfarabi, *The Gems of Wisdom*, in Collection, op. cit. pp. 115-125.

[34]Alfarabi, *The Gems of Wisdom*, in Collection, op. cit. pp. 115-125.

# THE PHILOSOPHY OF ALFARABI 15

The distinction between essence and existence in all created beings is brought in by Alfarabi to differentiate these substances from God, Who is absolutely simple and pure act. It reveals the true genius of Alfarabi, from whom St. Thomas drew the following:

> Omnis autem essentia vel quidditas intelligere potest sine hoc, quod aliquid intelligatur de esse suo facto: possum enim intelligere quid est homo, et tamen ignorare an esse habeat in rerum natura. Ergo patet, quod esse est aliud ab essentia vel quidditate, nisi forte sit aliqua res, cujus quidditas sit suum esse, et haec res non potest esse nisi una et prima.[35]

The finite, concrete thing is composed of two other principles, *matter* and *form*. *Matter* is nothing but a reality indeterminate as body. Because of its indetermination, it has only the aptitude to become, by virtue of the form, this or that body. *Form is* the principle that determines matter to be actually such a body. Neither matter can exist without form, nor form without matter. As long as the wood remains indifferent to being a cradle, it is a cradle in potentiality, and becomes a cradle in actuality the very moment it receives the form of a cradle. Furthermore, all finite beings are capable of receiving not only the form proper to them, but also the opposite. Matter and form are real elements or principles of being, and together they form a real and integral whole. If either were taken away, there would be no concrete thing at all. That is the reason why form is immanent in matter[36]

## THE FIRST PRINCIPLES

Closely related with the concept of being are the laws of

---

[35] "But every essence or quiddity can be understood without anything being known of its existence; for, I can understand what a man is, and yet not know whether it has existence in the natural order. Therefore, it is clear that existence is a different thing from essence or quiddity, unless perchance there be something whose essence is its very existence. And this thing must needs be one and the first." St. Thomas *De Ente et Essentia*, c. 4, tr. from the Latin by Clare C. Riedl, Chapter IV, p. 34.

[36] Alfarabi, *Political Regime*, 1 Arabic ed. p. 26.

thought and reality. If the concept of being is true, likewise the first principles are true. If the concept of being is based on reality, so are the first principles, which are not only the laws of thought, but also of reality. In fact, every first principle implies the fundamental idea of being.

*The principle of contradiction* is: It is impossible for the same thing to be and not to be at the same time.

*The principle of excluded middle* is: A thing either is or is not.

*The principle of causality* is thus formulated by Alfarabi: "Whatever exists after having not existed, must be brought into being by a cause; nothing (not-being) cannot be the cause of being."[37] Alfarabi arrived at the principle of causality through the analysis of the idea of motion. Motion or change involves a transition from not-being into being, from potentiality into actuality. And since not-being of itself cannot rise to being, we legitimately infer a something which causes the change. Change, like limitation, implies a something beyond itself, something to which change is due. That explains precisely the axiom, "Quidquid movetur, ab alio movetur", namely, that change implies a real and objective cause, of which Alfarabi and the Schoolmen felt very certain.

It is to be noted that Alfarabi, after having formulated the principle of causality in a philosophical way, wound up in mystic tendencies. He says,

> In the world of created things we do not find either produced impressions or free choice unless it is the result of a cause. Man cannot do a thing without relying on external causes, which are not of his choice, and these causes rely on the order, and the order on the decree, and the decree on the judgment, and the judgment comes from the commandment. And so everything is decreed.[38]

[37]Alfarabi, *The Gems of Wisdom*, in Collection, op. cit. p. 164.
[38]Alfarabi, *The Gems of Wisdom*, in Collection, op. cit. pp. 164-165.

## THE PHILOSOPHY OF ALFARABI

It should be noted, however, that apart from these mystic tendencies, Alfarabi is quite Aristotelian and deserves much credit and praise for passing on to us the following ontological truths:

Being cannot be defined. All subsequent philosophers, both Arabian and Scholastic, accepted it and made it their own.

Reality is being in becoming, actuality in potentiality, unity in difference. Hence, the different concepts of substance and accident, essence and existence, matter and form, cause and effect.

Concepts are not merely symbols or names, but on the contrary, they have real significance, and their primary function is to synthesize the many in the one. For him, therefore, concepts stand for the universal and the one, applicable to many and found in many (unum de multis et in multis).

Finally, every event must have a cause. This is a proposition that expresses the essential dependence of every effect on some cause. We can now see how the Ontology of Alfarabi treats of that which is, the nature of which is actuality in potentiality.

-2-

## METAPHYSICAL THEOLOGY

The Theodicy of Alfarabi, which considers God in Himself, does not differ much from the Christian both in the arguments proving God's existence, as well as in the exposition of the various attributes which constitute His nature. There are, undoubtedly, certain flaws here and there on some non-essential points, but as a whole I can say that one who reads his Theodicy gets the impression of reading an essay written by a Christian Father. In this section we shall deal at length, not only with the arguments by which Alfarabi proves God's existence, but also with each of the attributes of God as he considers them, in order to bring out the perfect similarity that exists between Christian Theodicy and the Theodicy of Alfarabi.

## THE KNOWABILITY OF GOD

One of the preliminary questions which confronted Alfarabi was whether or not God is knowable. On this question he could not make up his mind, and consequently, he was hesitant to give a definite answer. Perhaps his hesitancy arose from his failure to distinguish between what is simply self-evident and that which is self-evident to us. In fact, he says:

> It is very difficult to know what God is because of the limitation of our intellect and its union with matter. Just as light is the principle by which colors become visible, in like manner it would seem logical to say that a perfect light should produce a perfect vision. Instead, the very opposite occurs. A perfect light dazzles the vision. The same is true of God. The imperfect knowledge we have of God is due to the fact that He is infinitely perfect. That explains why His infinitely perfect being bewilders our mind. But if we could strip our nature of all that we call 'matter,' then certainly our knowledge of His being would be quite perfect.[39]

[39] Alfarabi, *Political Regime*, 1st Arabic ed. Cairo, Nile Press, pp. 12-13.

# THE PHILOSOPHY OF ALFARABI

In another place he says:

> God is knowable and unknowable, evident and hidden, and the best knowledge of Him is to know that He is something the human mind cannot thoroughly understand.[40]

A glance, however, into Alfarabi's later teaching leads us to the conclusion that he must have implicitly admitted the proposition, "God is", to be self-evident in itself, because he states repeatedly that God's essence is His existence, thus identifying the predicate with the subject. But since our mind is unable to understand the selfsame thing of both these terms, the implication is that Alfarabi must have come to the tacit conclusion that this proposition, "God is", is self-evident in itself, although not to us, and what is not evident to us can be demonstrated.[41] According to him, the knowledge of God is the object of philosophy, and the duty of man is to rise, as far as is humanly possible, up to the likeness of God.[42]

## PROOFS OF GOD'S EXISTENCE

The arguments brought forth by Alfarabi to prove that there is a God, are three. These will be placed side by side with those of St. Thomas in order to aid the reader in comparing them. He will thus see the great similarity between them.

| PROOFS ADDUCED BY ALFARABI | PROOFS ADDUCED BY ST. THOMAS |
|---|---|
| 1. The Proof of Motion. In this world there are things which are moved. Now, every object which is moved receives its motion from a mover. If the mover is itself moved, there must be another mover moving it, and after that still another and so on. But it is impossible to go onto infinity in the series of movers | It is certain and evident to our senses that in the world some things are in motion. Now, whatever is in motion is put in motion by another ... If that by which it is put in motion be itself put in motion, then this also must needs be put in motion by another, and that by another again. But this cannot go on to infinity. There- |

[40] Alfarabi, *The Gems of Wisdom*, in Collection, op. cit. p. 173.
[41] Alfarabi, *The Gems of Wisdom*, in Collection, op. cit. pp. 115-125.
[42] Alfarabi, *What Must Precede the Study of Philosophy*, in Collection, op. cit. n. 4, p. 62.

and things moved. Therefore, there must be an immovable mover, and this is God.⁴³

fore, it is necessary to arrive at a first mover, put in motion by no other; and this everyone understands to be God.⁴⁴

2. Proof of Efficient Cause.

In contemplating the changeable world, one sees that it is composed of beings which have a cause, and this cause, in turn, is the cause of another. Now, in the series of efficient causes it is not possible to proceed to infinity. For, if A were the cause of B, B of C, C of D, and so on, here A would be the cause of itself, which is not admissible. Therefore, outside the series of efficient causes, there must be an uncaused efficient cause, and this is God.⁴⁵

In the world of sense we find there is an order of efficient causes. There is no case known (neither is possible) in which a thing is found to be the efficient cause of itself ... Now, in efficient causes it is not possible to go on to infinity ... Therefore, it is necessary to admit a first efficient cause, to which everyone gives the name of God.⁴⁶

Another form of the same proof:

Transition from not-being to being demands an actual cause. This cause either has its essence identical with its existence or not. If it does, then being is uncaused. If it does not, then existence must be from another, and that from another, and so on until we arrive at a First Cause, whose essence differs in no way from its existence.⁴⁷

3. Proof of Contingence.

The third proof is based on the principle that all change must

We find in nature things that are possible to be and not to

---

⁴³Alfarabi, *The Sources of Questions*, in Collection, op. cit. n. 13, pp. 70-71.
⁴⁴St. Thomas, *Summa Theologica*, part I, Q. 2, Art. 3.
⁴⁵Alfarabi, *The Gems of Wisdom*, in Collection, op. cit. pp. 115-125.
⁴⁶St. Thomas, Ibid. op. cit.
⁴⁷Alfarabi, *The Sources of Questions*, in Collection, op. cit. n. 2, p. 65.

have a cause. To this effect Alfarabi makes a distinction between a necessary being and a contingent being. "Contingent beings," he says, "have had a beginning. Now, that which begins to exist must owe its existence to the action of a cause. This cause, in turn, either is or is not contingent. If it is contingent, it also must have received its existence by the action of another cause, and so on. But a series of contingent beings which would produce one another cannot proceed to infinity or move in a circle. Therefore, the series of causes and effects must arrive at a cause that holds its existence from itself, and this is the first cause (ens primum)."[48]

be ... But it is impossible for these always to exist ... Therefore, not all beings are merely possible, but there must exist something, the existence of which is necessary. But every necessary being either has its necessity caused by another or not. Now, it is impossible to go on to infinity in necessary things which have their necessity caused by another. Therefore, we cannot but postulate the existence of some being having of itself its own necessity, and not receiving it from another, but rather causing in others their necessity. This all men speak of as God.[49]

The different arguments brought forth by Alfarabi to prove God's existence are really so many statements of one and the same argument which is commonly called the "cosmological" argument. This argument derives its validity from the principle of causality. And if the principle of causality is validly used by the scientists to explain the phenomena of physics, likewise it must be regarded as validly employed by the philosopher to explain the universe. Hence, the cosmological argument is valid because the principle of causality is valid.

The proof of an immovable mover by Aristotle, which leads to the conclusion that God is a designer and not a creator, was improved and corrected by Alfarabi nearly three hundred years before St. Thomas was born. Starting out from the Aristotelian idea of change, Alfarabi was able to arrive at an Ens Primum to whom that change is due, while He Himself does not change, because He is pure act.

The proofs of causality and contingence as given by St. Thomas are merely a repetition of Alfarabi's proofs. This is said,

---

[48] Alfarabi, *The Sources of Questions*, in Collection, op. cit. n. 3, p. 66.
[49] St. Thomas, Ibid. op. cit.

not because of any bias against St. Thomas, but rather because this is evident to anyone after studying the works of both Alfarabi and of St. Thomas.

The main idea running through all the proofs of Alfarabi is being. That which begins to exist implies a self-existent being. A finite and contingent being, that is, a being which has not given itself existence, implies a Being that holds its existence from itself. A being which begins to exist must have a cause for its existence.

An analysis of the proofs adduced by Alfarabi shows how he was able to arrive at their formulation. In each of his three proofs he starts out from a fact, applies a principle, and arrives at the conclusion. The fact is *change, caused being* and *contingence*. The principle is: that which is moved, is moved by another; the effect implies a cause; the contingent implies the necessary. The conclusion is that God exists.

## HOW MAN ACQUIRES KNOWLEDGE OF GOD'S NATURE AND OF HIS ATTRIBUTES

Since man knows only what he finds out by his own senses and intelligence, it follows that he has no other way of knowing the divine nature except by observation. And observing the visible world, he perceives certain perfections and imperfections in it. To the first class belong such perfections as being, life, intelligence, truth, goodness and so on, which of themselves connote perfection. To the second class belong all imperfections as non-being, non-living, non-intelligence, which necessarily connote imperfection. While it cannot be said that God is non-living, non-intelligent, it can be said that He is infinitely good, intelligent and wise. While imperfections are removed from God, perfections can be attributed to Him eminently, namely, whatever positive being they express belongs to God as their cause in a much higher sense and in a more excellent way than to the creatures in which they exist. Another way of saying this is: given an infinite cause and finite effects, whatever pure perfection is discovered in the effects must first exist in the cause [Via Affirmationis], and at the same time whatever im-

# THE PHILOSOPHY OF ALFARABI

perfection is discovered in the effects must be excluded from the cause [Via Remotionis]. Alfarabi agrees with the foregoing explanation, saying that

> We can have some knowledge of the nature of God by means of a two-fold process: first, by exclusion [Via Remotionis], by which we remove from God whatever implies defect, as limitation, dependence, mutability; and second, by pre-eminence [Via Eminentiae], by which we attribute to God in an infinite degree all perfections, such as goodness, wisdom, etc.[50]

Concerning the method to be followed in determining God's nature, St. Thomas says exactly the same thing in the following words:

> We have some knowledge thereof (divine essence) by knowing what it is not: and we shall approach all the nearer to the knowledge thereof according as we shall be enabled to remove by our intellect a greater number of things therefrom.[51]

In another place St. Thomas says: "Quaelibet creatura potest in Deum venire tribus modis, scilicet, per causalitatem, remotionem, eminentiam."[52]

The following are the attributes of God as considered by Alfarabi and St. Thomas.

### (A) Process of Exclusion

| ATTRIBUTES CONSIDERED BY ALFARABI | ATTRIBUTES CONSIDERED BY ST. THOMAS |
|---|---|
| **SIMPLICITY OF GOD** | |
| God is simple because He is free from every kind of composition, physical or metaphysical. | There is no composition in God. For, in every composite thing there must needs be act and po- |

---

[50] Alfarabi, *The Knowledge of God*, in Traites inedits d'anciens philosophes arabes. Published by Malouf, Edde and Cheiko, 2nd Arabic ed., Beirut, 1911, pp. 21-22.

[51] St. Thomas, *Summa Contra Gentiles*, first bk. Tr. by the English Dominican Fathers, chap. XIV, p. 33.

[52] St. Thomas, *I Sent.*, III, quest. 1, a. 3.

Physical composition may be either substantial or accidental. It is substantial if the composite substance consists of body and soul, of matter and form. Now, an infinite being cannot be a substantial composite of matter and form, because this would mean that God results from the union of finite parts which would exist before Him in time, and therefore be the cause of His being. Nor can an accidental composition be attributed to the infinite, because this would imply a capacity for an increase in perfection, which the very notion of the infinite excludes. Therefore, there is not and cannot be any physical composition.53

Neither can there be that kind of composition known as metaphysical, which results from the union of two different concepts so referred to the same real thing that neither one by itself signifies the whole reality as meant by their union. Thus, every contingent being is a metaphysical composite of essence and existence. Essence, as such, in reference to a contingent being, implies its conceivableness or possibility, and abstracts from actual existence; while existence, as such, must be added to essence before we can speak of the being as actual. But the composite of essence and existence in a contingent being cannot be applied to the self-existent or infinite being in whom essence and existence are one. Therefore, there is no composition of essence and existence in God.55

tentiality ... But in God there is no potentiality. Therefore, in Him there is no composition ... Every composite is subsequent to its components. Therefore, the first being, namely God, has no component parts.54

Existence denotes a kind of actuality ... Now everything to which an act is becoming, and which is distinct from that act, is related thereto as potentiality to act ... Accordingly if the divine essence is distinct from its existence, it follows that His essence and existence are mutually related as potentiality and act. Now it has been proved that in God there is nothing of potentiality, and that He is pure act. Therefore God's essence is not distinct from His existence.56

---

53Alfarabi, *Political Regime.* Second Arabic ed. Cairo, Nile Press, p. 2.

54St. Thomas, *Summa Contra Gentiles.* First Bk., op. cit. Chap. XVIII, p. 39.

55Alfarabi, *The Gems of Wisdom*, in Collection, op. cit. pp. 115-125.

56St. Thomas, *Summa Contra Gentiles*, First Bk., Ch. XXII, p. 55.

# THE PHILOSOPHY OF ALFARABI

Nor can the composition of genus and difference, implied in the definition of man as a rational animal, be attributed to Him. For, God cannot be classified or defined, as contingent beings can. The reason is because there is not a single aspect in which He is perfectly similar to the finite, and consequently no genus in which He can be included.[57]

Wherefore it is likewise evident that God cannot be defined: since every definition is composed of genus and difference.[58]

## INFINITY OF GOD

**ALFARABI**

The uncaused being is infinite. For, if He were not, He would be limited, and therefore, caused, since the limit of a thing is the cause of it. But God is uncaused. Hence, it follows that the first being is infinite.[59]

**ST. THOMAS**

Being itself, considered absolutely, is infinite ... Hence if we take a thing with finite being, this being must be limited by some other thing which is in some way the cause of that being. Now there can be no cause of God's being, since He is necessary of Himself. Therefore He has infinite being, and Himself is infinite.[60]

## IMMUTABILITY OF GOD

God as the first cause is pure act, without the admixture of any potentiality, and for this reason He is not subject to any change.[61]

It is shown that God is altogether immutable. First, because it was shown above that there is some first being, whom we call God; and that this first being must be pure act, without the admixture of any potentiality, for the reason that, absolutely, potentiality is posterior to act. Now everything which is in any way changed, is in some way in potentiality. Hence it is evident that it is impossible for God to be in any way changeable.[62]

---

[57] Alfarabi, *The Gems of Wisdom*, in Collection, op. cit. p. 132.
[58] St. Thomas, *Summa Contra Gentiles.* First Bk., Ch. XXV, p. 61.
[59] Alfarabi, *Political Regime.* Second Arabic ed. Nile Press, p. 7.
[60] St. Thomas, *Summa Contra Gentiles.* First Bk., Ch. XLIII, p. 96.
[61] Alfarabi, *Political Regime*, op. cit. p. 7.
[62] St. Thomas, *Summa Theologica.* Part I, Q. 9, Art. 1 ad 1, pp. 91-92.

## THE PHILOSOPHY OF ALFARABI
## UNITY OF GOD

### ALFARABI

God is only one. For, if there were two gods, they would have to be partly alike and partly different: in which case, however, the simplicity of each would be destroyed. In other words, if there were two gods, there would necessarily have to be some difference and some identity between them; the differential and the common element would constitute the parts of the essence of each one, and these parts, in turn, would be the cause of all; and then, not God, but His parts, would be the first being.

If there was anything equal to God, then He would cease to be the fullness of being, for fullness implies impossibility of finding anything of its kind. For instance, the fullness of power means inability of finding identical power anywhere else; the fullness of beauty means inability of finding identical beauty. Likewise if the first being possesses the fullness of being, this means that it is impossible to find anyone or anything identical with Him. Therefore, there is one infinite being, only one God.63

God is one, because He is free from all quantitative divisions. One means undivided. He who is indivisible in substance is one in essence.67

### ST. THOMAS

If there be two things, both of which are of necessity, they must needs agree in the intention of the necessity of being. It follows, therefore, that they must be differentiated by something added either to one or to both of them; and consequently that either one is composite, or both. Now no composite exists necessarily *per se*. Therefore there cannot possibly be several things each of which exists necessarily; and consequently neither can there be several gods.64

God comprehends in Himself the whole perfection of being. If then many gods existed, they would necessarily differ from each other. Something therefore would belong to one, which did not belong to another ... So it is impossible for many gods to exist.65

God is existence itself. Consequently He must contain within Himself the whole perfection of being ... It follows therefore that the perfection of no one thing is wanting to God.66

Since one is an undivided being, if anything is supremely one it must be supremely being, and supremely undivided. Now both of these belong to God. Hence it is manifest that God is one in the supreme degree.68

---

63 Alfarabi, *Political Regime*, op. cit. pp. 3-5.
64 St. Thomas, *Summa Contra Gentiles*. First Bk., Ch. XLII, p. 90.
65 St. Thomas, *Summa Theologica*. Part I, Q. 11, Art. 3, pp. 116-117.
66 St. Thomas, *Summa Theologica*. Part I, Q. 4, Art. 2, p. 48.
67 Alfarabi, Id. op. cit. pp. 7-8.
68 St. Thomas, *Summa Theologica*. Part I, Q. 11, Art. 4, p. 118.

## (B) Process of Pre-eminence

### GOD IS INTELLIGENT

**ALFARABI**

God is intelligent. A thing is intelligent because it exists without matter. Now, God is absolutely immaterial. Therefore, He is intelligent.[69]

God knows Himself perfectly. If there is anything that would keep God from knowing Himself, that would certainly be matter. But God is absolutely immaterial. Hence it follows that He knows Himself fully, because His intellect is His essence.

That which by its essence is intellect in act, is, too, by its very essence intelligible in act. Now, the divine intellect is always intellect in act, because if it were not so, then it would be in potentiality with respect to its object; and this is impossible. Just exactly the opposite occurs in man. The human intellect is not always in act. Man knows himself in act after knowing himself potentially. The reason for this is that man's intellect is not his essence. Hence, what he knows does not belong to him by essence.[71]

**ST. THOMAS**

A thing is intelligent from the fact of its being without matter. Now it was shown above that God is absolutely immaterial. Therefore He is intelligent.[70]

That which by its nature is severed from matter and from material conditions, is by its very nature intelligible. Now every intelligible is understood according as it is actually one with the intelligent; and God is Himself intelligent, as we have proved. Therefore since He is altogether immaterial, and is absolutely one with Himself, He understands Himself most perfectly.

A thing is actually understood through the unification of the intellect in act and the intelligible in act. Now the divine intellect is always intellect in act ... Since the divine intellect and the divine essence are one, it is evident that God understands Himself perfectly: for God is both His own intellect and His own essence.[72]

---

[69] Alfarabi, Id., op. cit. p. 8.

[70] St. Thomas, *Summa Contra Gentiles.* First Bk., Ch. XLIV, p. 100.

[71] Alfarabi, *Political Regime*, p. 8-9.

[72] St. Thomas, *Summa Contra Gentiles.* First Bk., Ch. XLVII, p. 105.

## GOD KNOWS ALL THINGS THROUGH KNOWLEDGE OF HIMSELF

### ALFARABI

It must not be said that God derives His knowledge of things from the things themselves, but rather it must be said that He knows things through His essence. By looking at His essence, He sees everything. Hence, knowing His essence is the cause of His knowing other things.[73]

### ST. THOMAS

So we say that God sees Himself in Himself, because He sees Himself through His essence; and He sees other things, not in themselves, but in Himself; inasmuch as His essence contains the similitude of things other than Himself.[74]

## GOD IS TRUTH

Truth follows being, namely, truth and being coincide. But God is the supreme being. Therefore, He is the supreme truth. Truth is the conformity of the intellect and thing. But in God intellect and object of thought are one and the same.[75]

Truth and being are mutually consequent upon one another; since the True is when that is said to be which is, and that not to be, which is not. Now God's being is first and most perfect. Therefore His truth is also first and supreme... Truth is in our intellect through the latter being equated to the thing understood. Now the cause of equality is unity. Since then in the divine intellect, intellect and thing understood are absolutely the same, His truth must be the first and supreme truth.[76]

## GOD IS LIFE

Just as we call ourselves living beings, because we have a nature capable of sensation or understanding, in like manner God, whose intellect is His essence, must have life in the most perfect degree.[77]

Wherefore that being whose act of understanding is its very nature, must have life in the most perfect degree.[78]

---

[73] Alfarabi, *The Gems of Wisdom*, in Collection, op. cit., p. 170.

[74] St. Thomas, *Summa Theologica*. Part I, Q. 14, Art. 5, p. 190.

[75] Alfarabi, *Political Regime*, op. cit., pp. 10-11.

[76] St. Thomas, *Summa Contra Gentiles*. First Bk., Ch. LXII, pp. 131-132.

[77] Alfarabi, *Political Regime*, op. cit., p. 11.

[78] St. Thomas, *Summa Theologica*. Part I, Q. 18, Art. 3, p. 255.

The foregoing is but a summary of Alfarabi's teaching about God and His attributes. My conclusion is that his Theodicy shows a scholarly, closely reasoned work. For, he has given us a carefully worked out treatise on the question of God's existence and His attributes. On the question of God's existence, he improved the Aristotelian proof of the first mover, adding to it two other proofs, that of efficient causes and of contingence. On the other hand, the attributes of God are dealt with so perfectly from the Christian viewpoint that the whole topic seems to have been written by a Christian Father, rather than by a Mohammedan. That Alfarabi's Theodicy exerted a great influence on Medieval thinkers is evident, because, upon comparing the teachings of Alfarabi with those of St. Thomas, we see without doubt the influence of the former on the latter, but not viceversa.

## -3-

## METAPHYSICAL COSMOLOGY

## RELATION OF GOD TO THE WORLD

That God exists is a proven truth; that the world was made is another truth. The most arduous question, however, which man tries to solve is this: What relation is there between God and the world, the Infinite and the finite? What connection is there between God and matter? Is there a bridge thrust from one side to the other over which God might pass to give matter a determinate form? The dualism of spirit and matter, infinite and finite, constitutes the cosmological problem of Metaphysics. In an effort to explain the action of God on matter, Alfarabi placed the intellects of the Spheres between God and the world. Thus, he made the many proceed from the One by *emanation*. His theory is as follows:

From the First Being (the One) comes forth the first intellect called the First Caused. From the first intellect thinking of the First Being flows forth a second intellect and a sphere. From the second intellect proceeds a third intellect and a sphere. The process goes on in necessary succession down to the lowest sphere, that of the moon. From the moon flows forth a pure intellect, called *active intellect*. Here end the separate intellects, which are, by essence, intellects and intelligibles. Here is reached the lower end of the supersensible world (the world of ideas of Plato).

These ten intellects, together with the nine spheres, constitute the second principle of Being. The active intellect, which is a bridge between heaven and earth, is the third principle. Finally matter and form appear as the fifth and sixth principles, and with these is closed the series of spiritual existences.

Only the first of these principles is unity, while the others represent plurality. The first three principles, God, the intellects of the spheres and the active intellect, remain spirit *per se,* namely, they are not bodies, nor are they in direct relation with bodies; neither are the last three (soul, form, matter) bodies by themselves, but they are only united to them.

There are six kinds of bodies: the celestial, the rational animal, the irrational animal, the vegetal, the mineral and the four elements (air, water, fire, earth). All of these principles and bodies taken together make up the universe.[79]

The theory of separate intellects such as taught by Alfarabi and other Arabian philosophers is simply a mixture of Aristotelian theories on the motion of heavenly spheres (Met. XII, cap. 7 and 8) and of the neo-Platonic doctrine of emanation. The student of philosophy may be surprised to hear such a strange and ridiculous theory. But, should he delve into its origin, he would certainly find that the belief in the animation of stars is just a particular case of what men formerly believed, namely, the animation of nature.

## ETERNITY OF MATTER AND ETERNITY OF THE WORLD

Alfarabi firmly believed that the world is the workmanship of an eternal, intelligent being; and thus God is the first principle or the efficient cause. He also believed that God, in order to make the world, must have had materials to work upon. From this he inferred that an eternal, uncreated matter must have been the material cause of the universe. But this matter, he be-

---

[79] Alfarabi, *The Sources of Questions,* in Collection, op. cit. n. 6, pp. 67-75

lieved, had no form, though it contained many forms in potentiality. This is what he says:

> When people say that God created the world, they simply mean that God produced the world out of matter by clothing it with a determinate form. The world is certainly God's work, and though it comes after Him as a world-form, yet it is equal to Him in time or eternal, insofar as He could not begin to work on it in time. The reason for this is that God is to the world exactly what a cause is to its effect. Since the cause in this case is inseparable from the effect, it follows that He could not, in a given moment, start making it. For, if He could, that would simply imply imperfection on His part while He had been trying to achieve His goal. This, of course, is incompatible with the absolute perfection of God.[80]

The eternity of the world and of matter as held by Alfarabi and Avicenna was rejected by Averroes and Maimonides, who taught the "creatio mundi ex nihilo." From the latter St. Thomas borrowed the proposition that the world was created from nothing.

## DUALISM OF GOOD AND EVIL

According to neo-Platonists, the dualism of spirit and matter gives rise to the existence of two principles, the principle of good and the principle of evil. For them, evil is linked with matter. Fortunately, the neo-Platonic teaching on this problem did not have much influence on Alfarabi. For, he says:

> God's providence is exercised over all things. Hence, whatever happens in the world is not to be attributed to chance. Evil is under divine control and is united to corruptible things. That evil exists in the world is good accidentally, because if it did not exist, a great deal of good in the world would never come about.[81]

In conclusion, it should be noted that Alfarabi's Metaphys-

---

[80] Alfarabi, *The Sources of Questions*, in Collection, op. cit. n. 6, pp. 67-68.
 See also: Alfarabi, *A Letter in Reply to Certain Questions*, in Collection, op. cit. n. p. 93.

[81] Alfarabi, *The Sources of Questions* in Collection, op. cit., n. 22, p. 75.

ical Cosmology is not original at all, but rather it is a mixture of Aristotelian theories (motion of the spheres, eternity of matter) and of neo-Platonic emanation.

## -4-

## METAPHYSICAL PSYCHOLOGY

In this part Alfarabi discusses the various problems concerning the human soul.

### THE SOUL IS A BEING QUITE DISTINCT FROM THE BODY

Alfarabi holds that the human soul is essentially distinct from the body, simply because he accepts the Aristotelian definition of the soul as the entelechy or the substantial form of the body. By this he means that the soul is the principle of life in man, a principle by which he thinks, feels and wills, and by which his body is animated. [82] This is also borne out by the fact that

> Man is composed of two principles, body and soul. The body is composed of parts, limited by space, measurable, divisible; while the soul is free from all bodily qualities. The former is a product of the created world, while the latter is simply the product of the last separate intellect of the supersensible world.[83]

### SPIRITUALITY OF THE HUMAN SOUL

The soul of man is not only simple and indivisible, but it is also spiritual. That is, it is in itself independent of matter and can subsist apart from the body. He says:

> The spirituality of the soul is demonstrated by its specific operations, which are intellection and volition. The operation of a being is according to the nature of the being itself (*Actio sequitur esse*). Now, intellect and will may attain to the abstract and immaterial; therefore, the soul itself must also be independent of matter.

---

[82]Alfarabi, *A Letter in Reply to Certain Questions*, in Collection, op. cit., n. 33, p. 108.

[83]Alfarabi, *The Gems of Wisdom*, in Collection, op. cit., p. 145.

In addition to this, he says:

> *Omne agens agit sibi simile*, which means that the effect must resemble its cause, for the soul can give to its operations only what it has itself. Therefore, the spiritual operations of the soul give us true knowledge of the nature of the soul itself.[84]

## IMMORTALITY OF THE HUMAN SOUL

Alfarabi held that the human soul cannot exist before the body, as Plato had said. Nor can it migrate from one body to another, as taught by the author of *Metempsychosis*.[85] However, it is very doubtful whether Alfarabi believed in the immortality of the human soul. For, he wrote passages for and against immortality. Against immortality we find the following passages:

> The only thing that survives the dissolution of the body is the active intellect, the *dator formarum* which is incorruptible.[86]

And in his lost commentary on the Nicomachean Ethics, he is reported by Averroes to have said that

> The supreme good of man is in this life, and anything meant to attain it in the life to come is but folly; it is an old wives' tale.

In fact, toward the end of his treatise on the Passive Intellect and its union with the Active, Averroes quotes Alfarabi as saying in the commentary mentioned above that

> Man's supreme good in this life is to attain knowledge. But to say that man after death becomes a separate form is an old wives' tale; for whatever is born and dies is incapable of becoming immortal.

This statement of Alfarabi brought much reproof on him, and

[84]Alfarabi, *The Gems of Wisdom*, in Collection, op. cit., p. 145.
[85]Alfarabi, *The Sources of Questions*, in Collection, op. cit., n. 22, p. 75.
[86]Alfarabi, *The Sources of Questions*, in Collection, op. cit. n. 21, pp. 74-75.

for it Immanuel Ben Solomon, in his *Final Judgment*, consigns him to the infernal regions.[87]

However, in contrast with these passages, we find one in favor of immortality. "After death," he says, "the human soul will be happy or unhappy according to its merits or demerits."[88] In the face of these statements for and against the immortality of the soul, it is difficult indeed to tell whether or not Alfarabi believed in it. Most probably he did not.

---

[87] Cf. *Mahberot* by Immanuel. Ch. XXVIII, Berlin. P. 251.
[88] Alfarabi, *The Sources of Questions*, in Collection, op. cit., n. 22, p. 75.

## Chapter III

## *PSYCHOLOGY*

## *GENERAL OUTLINE OF THE POWERS OF THE SOUL*

"The human soul," says Alfarabi, "is a unity in difference. This means that the soul is one, and that its unity is the basis for certain differences or powers. The powers of the soul are multiple but can be reduced to three kinds: vegetative, sensitive and intellective."[89] Hence the following schema:

The Soul is: Vegetative, Sensitive, Intellective.

1. The Vegetative has three Powers:
   — Nutritive
   — Augmentative
   — Generative

2. The Sensitive has two Powers:

   (a) Powers of Knowledge:
   — External sensible (five external senses)
   — Internal sensible (Imagination, Memory, Estimative power)

   (b) Powers of Action:
   — Sensitive (Concupiscible and Irascible)
   — Locomotive

3. The Intellective has two Powers:

   (a) Powers of Knowledge:
   — Perceptive (knowledge of the individual)
   — Abstractive (knowledge of the universal) is obtained through the four Intellects:
   Passive Intellect
   Active Intellect
   Actual Intellect
   Acquired Intellect

   (b) Power of Action
   Intellective (the will)

---

[89] Alfarabi, *The Gems of Wisdom*, in Collection, op. cit., pp. 147-152. See also *Political Regime*, op. cit., p. 47-51; *The Sources of Questions*, in Collection, op. cit., n. 20, p. 74.

## -1-

## THE POWERS OF KNOWLEDGE

## SENSE - KNOWLEDGE

In the exposition of the theory of knowledge we shall compare the theory of Alfarabi with that of St. Thomas for the purpose of helping the reader discover at a glance the similarity and the difference between them.

### ALFARABI

Every idea comes from sense-experience according to the adage: "There is nothing in the intellect that has not first been in the senses." The mind is like a smooth tablet on which nothing is written . It is the senses that do all the writing on it. The senses are five: sight, hearing, smell, taste and touch. Each of these has a proper sensible thing for its object. In every sensation the sense receives the form or species of sensible things without the matter, just as wax receives the form of a seal without any of the matter of it.[90]

### ST. THOMAS

Now, sense is a passive power, and is naturally changed by the exterior sensible. Wherefore the exterior cause of such change is what is directly perceived by the sense, and according to the diversity of that exterior cause are the sensitive powers diversified. Now, change is of two kinds, one natural and the other spiritual. Natural change takes place by the form of the changer being received, according to its natural existence, into the thing changed, as heat is received into the thing heated. Whereas spiritual change takes place by the form of the changer being received, according to a spiritual mode of existence, into the thing changed, as the form of color is received into the pupil which does not thereby become colored. Now, for the operation of the senses, a spiritual change is required, whereby an intention of the sensible form is effected in sensible organ.[91]

---

[90] Alfarabi, *The Gems of Wisdom*, in Collection, op. cit., p. 149; see also: Alfarabi, *Political Regime*, op. cit., pp. 47-51.

[91] St. Thomas, *Summa Theologica*. Part I, Third No. (QQ. LXXV-CXIX) - Q. LXXVIII, Art. 3, p. 80. Tr. by the English Dominican Fathers.

# THE PHILOSOPHY OF ALFARABI

If Alfarabi had worked out more in detail the theory of sense-knowledge, he probably would have brought out not only the physical factor, but also the psychical. For, he seems to take for granted the following factors which bring about sensation proper. First, without the organs of the several senses, there can be no sensation. We cannot see without eyes, nor hear without ears. A sense organ is a *potentia passiva,* the actuation of which is due to a stimulus, and ultimately to an object. Second, when the object acts upon the sense-organ, it must produce therein a modification which is like to itself, and generally called sensible species. In receiving the sensible species, the sense passes from potentia passiva to act. Hence, when sensible species are produced in a sentient organism, they must produce a corresponding reaction which we call sensation

## ALFARABI

The sensations we have once experienced are not utterly dead. They can reappear in the form of images. The power by which we revive a past sensible experience without the aid of any physical stimulus is called imagination (el-motakhayilah).

The power by which we combine and divide images is called the cogitative (el-mofakarah). If we were limited merely to the experience of our actual sensations, we would have only the present, and with it there would be no intellectual life at all. But fortunately we are endowed with the power of calling back a former experience, and this is called memory (el-hafizah- el-zakirah).

## ST. THOMAS

For the retention and preservation of these forms (sensible forms), the phantasy or imagination is appointed; which are the same, for phantasy or imagination is as it were a storehouse of forms received through the senses. Furthermore, for the apprehension of intentions which are not received through the senses, the estimative power is appointed: and for the preservation thereof, the memorative power, which is a storehouse of such like intentions.[92]

Finally, among the internal senses Alfarabi mentions instinct or el-uahm (the estimative power of the Scholastics), by which animals seek what is useful to them and avoid what is harmful. "It is by this faculty," he says, "that the sheep knows that the

---

[92] St. Thomas, *Summa Theologica.* Part I, Third No. Q. LXXVIII, Art. 4, p. 85.

wolf is his enemy and that the little lambs need its care and attention."[93]

## PERCEPTIVE KNOWLEDGE AND PERCEPTS CONTRASTED WITH CONCEPTS

If while hard at work writing, I smell something sweet but cannot tell where the sweet odor is coming from, I am said to have a sensation of smell. If I refer that "something sweet" to a rose on the table, then I have a percept of the smell of the rose. From this it follows that sensation is not knowledge (sentire est nondum scire).

Man's first knowledge, according to Alfarabi, is a percept. A percept is a knowledge of the individual, free from abstraction; it is individuality without universality. It comes after sensation, but prior to a concept (knowledge of the universal). Literally he says: "There is one part of the soul in which occurs the first knowledge, a knowledge free from abstraction, and which apprehends the principles of science immediately and without reflection."[94]

That a percept (knowledge of the individual) comes first, is proved by the fact that our mind must have the individual before abstracting from it the universal. Hence, there is nothing in the intellect that has not been first in sense-perception.

But a percept is simply incomplete knowledge. To know the individual completely we must see it and understand it in relation to other individuals, which is like saying that we must conceive it and think of it.

For Alfarabi, what is commonly called thought or concept seems to represent something like the concrete universal, something like the universal existing in the particular concrete thing.

[93] Alfarabi, *The Gems of Wisdom*, in Collection, op. cit., p. 152.
[94] Alfarabi, *The Intellect and the Intelligible*, in Collection, op. cit. n. 3, p. 47.

# THE PHILOSOPHY OF ALFARABI

This is easily inferred from his definition of the universal as "Unum de multis et in multis." By the word "Unum" he means that the universality, that common something, is abstracted from the concrete thing (percept); and by the words "de multis et in multis" he means that the universality is to be applied to concrete cases and is contained within them.

That Alfarabi holds universality in concreteness as peculiar features of the concept is seen from the fact that he does not admit in its absolute sense the aphorism "singulare sentitur, universale intelligitur." He rather believes that, while by its matter the particular concrete thing is the object of sense-perception, yet by its form or essence, it is in the intellect, too. On the other hand, though the universal, as such, is in the intellect, yet it is also in sense-perception insofar as it is immanent in the individual.[95]

## ABSTRACTIVE KNOWLEDGE

All our intellectual powers are grouped under our common name "intellect," by which we think, judge and reason. Alfarabi points out the various meanings of the term "intellect" as used in common speech and in philosophy proper. In everyday language "an intelligent man," he says, "means a man of reliable judgment, who knows what he has to do as right and what he has to avoid as wrong, and thus is distinguished from a crafty man who employs his mind in devising evil expedients."[96] He continues:

> Theologians use the term "intellect" to denote the faculty which tests the validity of statements, either approving them as true or rejecting them as false. Hence, by "intellect" they mean the faculty which perceives the truths of common evidence.[97]

In Analytics Aristotle uses the term "intellect" to denote

---

[95] Albertus Magnus, An. post. I,. 1, 3.
[96] Alfarabi, *The Intellect and the Intelligible,* in Collection, op, cit. n. 1, pp. 45-46.
[97] Alfarabi, Ibid. op. cit. n. 2, p. 47.

the faculty by which man attains to the certain knowledge of axioms and general abstract truths without the need of proof. This faculty is that part of the soul in which occurs the first knowledge (sense percept), and which is thereby able to lay hold of the premises of speculative science.[98]

In the book of Ethics Aristotle mentions an intellect of moral truths, and this is, for Alfarabi, that part of the soul in which moral experience, as we call it, takes place and by which we try to distinguish the acts to be done from those to be avoided.[99]

Finally comes the intellect spoken of in the *Anima,* and is the intellect proper. This is of two kinds: the *speculative intellect* is an apprehensive power relating to what is above itself, while the *practical intellect* is a motive power referring to what is below itself, namely, to the sensitive world that it must govern. The speculative intellect, as treated by Alfarabi, consists of four faculties or parts of the soul: the passive and active intellects, the acquired intellect and the actual intellect.

## ALFARABI

The passive intellect or aql hayulani is in potentiality to things intelligible. It passes from potentiality to act when it separates mentally the essence from its individuating notes. This essence, abstracted from the individuals, becomes actually the intelligible form or species which is one and the same as the intellect in act.

When forms existing in matter outside the soul become actually intelligible, their existence as

## ST. THOMAS

The human intellect is in potentiality with regard to things intelligible, and is at first like a clean tablet on which nothing is written. This is made clear from the fact that at first we are only in potentiality to understand and afterwards we are made to understand actually. And so it is evident that with us to understand is in a way to be passive, and consequently the intellect is a passive power.[100]

Nothing is reduced from potentiality to act except by something in act; as the senses are

[98] Alfarabi, Ibid. op. cit. n. 3, p. 47.
[99] Alfarabi, Ibid. op. cit. n. 4, pp. 47-48.
[100] St. Thomas, *Summa Theologica.* Part I, Third No. (QQ. LXXV-CXIX), - Q. LXXIX, Art. 2, p. 92.

actually intelligible is not the same as forms existing in matter. For forms existing in matter (individualized concretely) are associated with the various categories of time and place, quantity and quality, but they are stripped of these individuating conditions the moment they become actually intelligible.101

The active intellect, or aql faal of which Aristotle speaks in the Anima III, is immaterial....it causes the passive intellect to pass from potentiality to act, and makes the intelligible in potentiality intelligible in act.

The active intellect is related to the passive as the sun is to the eye. The eye is in potentiality to see while it is dark, but it sees actually as soon as light shines. The same is to be said of both the passive and active intellect.

The active intellect shines a kind of light upon the passive, by which the passive becomes actual, (aql bilfil) and the intelligible in potentiality becomes intelligible in act. Furthermore, the active intellect is a separate substance, which, by lighting up the phantasms, makes them to be actually intelligible.104

made actual by what is actually sensible. We must therefore assign on the part of the intellect, some power, to make things actually intelligible, by the abstraction of the species from material conditions. And such is the necessity for an active intellect.102

The intellectual soul is indeed actually immaterial, but it is in potentiality to determinate species. On the contrary, phantasms are actual images of certain species, but are immaterial in potentiality. Wherefore nothing prevents one and the same soul, inasmuch as it is actually immaterial, having one power by which it makes things actually immaterial, by abstraction from the conditions of individual matter: which power is called the active intellect; and another power, receptive of such species, which is called the passive intellect by reason of its being in potentiality to such species.103

## ALFARABI

The acquired intellect or aql mustafad is simply the actual intellect developed under the inspiration of the active intellect. Albertus Magnus calls it "Intellectus adeptus"106

## ST. THOMAS

Not only does the active intellect throw light on the phantasm; it does more. By its own power it abstracts the intelligible species from the phantasm. It throws light on the phantasm,

---

101Alfarabi, *The Intellect and the Intelligible*, op. cit., n. 5, pp. 49-54.
102St. Thomas, *Summa Theologica*, Part I, Third No., Q. LXXIX, Art. 3, p. 94.
103St. Thomas, *Summa Theologica*, Part I, Third No., Q. LXXIX, Art. 4, ad. 4, p. 98.
104Alfarabi, *The Intellect and the Intelligible*, op. cit., n. 6, pp. 54-56.
106With regard to the acquired intellect, see Albertus Magnus, *Summa Theol.*, parag. II, Tract. XIII, Quaest. LXXVIII, Membr. 3.

Alfarabi's theory may be summed up as follows: the intellect, in its primitive state, is a power of the soul. Since it has only a potential existence, he calls it "aql hayulani", the material intellect. For, like matter, it has the capacity for taking on a new form. In fact, the material or passive intellect passes from potentiality to actuality when it abstracts the essence from the individuals. But what is the force that causes the passive intellect to pass from potentiality to act? It is, according to Alfarabi, the active intellect, a separate substance emanating from God which is able to awaken the latent power in man and arouse it to activity.

because, just as the sensitive part acquires a greater power by its conjunction with the intellectual part, so by the power of the active intellect the phantasms are made more fit for the abstraction therefrom of intelligible intentions. Furthermore, the active intellect abstracts the intelligible species from the phantasm, forasmuch as by the power of the active intellect we are able to disregard the conditions of individuality, and to take into our consideration the specific nature, the image of which informs the passive intellect.[105]

St. Thomas' theory boils down to this: to abstract the essence and to perceive it are two acts specifically distinct; therefore they demand two distinct powers. Hence the soul requires one power which renders the essences of sensible things actually intelligible by stripping them of their material conditions in which they exist: which power is called the active intellect; and another power by which it comprehends the intelligible: this is called the passive intellect because of its being in potentiality to all intelligibles.

[105] St. Thomas, *Summa Theologica*, Part I, Third Number, Q. LXXXV, Art. 1, ad. 4, p. 183.

## -2-

## POWERS OF ACTION

### SENSITIVE APPETITE

"By powers of action," says Alfarabi, "are meant those powers which have action or movement for their object, and they are all grouped under the name of 'appetite.'" A general law rules our appetitive powers: "Nil volitum quin fuerit praecognitum." Appetite follows knowledge. For, appetite can never operate unless something is known and presented to it. Appetite may be moved either by the sense or by the intellect. If the appetite is moved by the sense, it becomes sensitive appetite. This is simply a tendency to good perceived by the senses.

Now, the sensitive appetite is divided into two powers, the concupiscible appetite and the irascible appetite. Concupiscible appetite (shahuaniat) is a power by which the animal is led to seek what is useful to it, and to shun what is harmful. Irascible appetite (Gadibat) is a power by which the animal is aroused to acquire a good that is difficult to attain, and to remove any evil that would prevent its attainment. By his concupiscible appetite a dog seeks proper food and avoids what is injurious; by his irascible appetite he is angered and attacks the animal that tries to deprive him of his food.

The manifestations of the concupiscible appetite are called concupiscible passions, and those of the irascible appetite are called irascible passions.

Alfarabi characterizes the nature of the sensitive appetite by saying that

> it is accompanied by a physical, bodily change. Thus, for instance, when one is aroused by a great desire to see something, he looks up and stares at the thing. The

looking up and the staring represent the bodily change.¹⁰⁷

## INTELLECTIVE APPETITE

If the appetite is moved by the intellect, it becomes intellective appetite, or will, and through it man attains his perfection and happiness. Of this Alfarabi says:

> The will is not to be confused with freedom (the power of choice). Freedom can choose only what is possible, while the will can choose also the impossible. The latter is well exemplified in a man who does not will to die. Therefore, the will is more general than freedom, and for this reason all freedom is will, but not all will is freedom.¹⁰⁸

---

¹⁰⁷Alfarabi, *Political Regime*, op. cit., p. 65. See also pp. 50-51.

¹⁰⁸Alfarabi, *A Letter in Reply to Certain Questions*, in Collection, op. cit., n. 31, pp. 107-108.

# PART III

PRACTICAL PHILOSOPHY

# CHAPTER IV

## ETHICS

### ACTIONS—GOOD, BAD, INDIFFERENT

On the subject of human actions Alfarabi says:

> The end of human actions is happiness. Happiness is something all men desire. The voluntary actions by which man attains the end of his existence are called good, and from them proceed the habits of doing good, known as virtues; while the voluntary actions which prevent man from attaining his end are called evil, and from them flow the habits of doing evil, known as vices. Good actions deserve reward, whereas bad actions deserve punishment.[109]

And he continues:

> In addition to good and bad actions there are actions that are indifferent. These possess a morality without significance to merit or demerit, and because of this they are called indifferent or amoral.[110]

Finally, man will attain full happiness only when he becomes free from the obstacles of the body.

Beyond these fundamental ideas we know very little of Alfarabi's Ethics, simply because his commentary on the *Nicomachean Ethics,* which represents his ethical thought, has been lost. However, these few ideas show perfectly well the general trend of his thought.

---

[109] Alfarabi, *Political Regime,* op. cit., pp. 66-67. See also *A Letter in Reply to Certain Questions,* n. 30, p. 107.

[110] With regard to indifferent acts, see Alfarabi, *The Knowledge of God,* in traitès inèdits d'anciens philosophes arabes, published by Malouf, Edde and Cheikho, Second Arabic ed. Beirut, 1911. P. 23.

# CHAPTER V

## POLITICAL SOCIETY

> Man needs the help of his fellowmen to attain the perfection proper to his nature. Unlike the brute, man is not equipped by nature with all that is necessary for the preservation and development of his being. It is only through society that he finds a complete satisfaction of his physical, intellectual and moral needs. Hence, it follows, that society is natural to man.

These are Alfarabi's words. And according to him society is either perfect or imperfect. Perfect society is of three kinds: the highest, the intermediate and the lowest. The highest is the whole inhabited earth coming under one political organization. The intermediate is a nation occupying a specific place of the inhabited earth. The lowest is a city which represents a fraction of the territory of a nation.

Imperfect society is of three kinds: the village, the suburb of a city and the home. These are merely steps leading to the organization of the state.[111]

## DESCRIPTION OF THE MODEL STATE

Alfarabi describes the organization of a model state in these words:

> Just as the world is one harmonious whole ruled by the highest authority of God; just as the stars and the sublunar world are linked up and follow one another; just as the human soul is one in different powers; just as the human body is an organized whole moved by the heart; in like manner the state is to be regulated and patterned after these noble models.
>
> In the model state there must be a hierarchy of rulers coming under the control of a supreme head or prince. This prince, head of the model state or of the whole

[111] Alfarabi, *Political Regime*, op. cit. pp. 77-80.

## THE PHILOSOPHY OF ALFARABI 51

> earth, must possess certain traits: great intelligence, excellent memory, eloquence, firmness without weakness, firmness in the achievement of good, love for justice, love for study, love for truth, aversion to falsehood, temperance in food, drink and enjoyments, and contempt for wealth.
>
> All these traits must be found in one man alone placed in charge of directing the complicated machinery of the state. In case all these traits cannot be found in one man alone, then inquiry should be made to determine whether there are two or more who possess the required traits jointly. If there are two, they should both rule the model state. If there are three, then these three should rule. If more are needed, more should rule.[112]

Thus the government by one man alone winds up in an aristocratic republic.

He continues:

> Opposed to the model state are: the ignorant state, the perverted state and the mistaken state. The ignorant state is the state that has no knowledge of true happiness, and very often exchanges it for health, wealth and pleasure. Thus, it is the ignorant state which has for its end the acquisition of things, such as food, clothing and shelter; it is the ignorant state which has for its end the enjoyment of eating and drinking, sensual pleasures, amusements and games; it is the ignorant state which has for its end the seeking of praise and the making of a name; it is the ignorant state which believes in false liberty, by which everyone can do as he pleases; it is the ignorant state which pursues imperialism as a national policy, namely, the will of conquering people and nations by fire and sword.
>
> The perverted state is the state that maintains a conduct similar to that of the ignorant state, even though it knows what is true happiness and perfection.
>
> The mistaken state is the state that has wrong ideas about God and happiness.[113]

Alfarabi, in his conception of the state, shows a mystico-philosophical belief in the absorption of the human spirit into the world spirit, and finally into God. In fact, he says:

> The goal of the model state is not only to procure the

---
[112]Alfarabi, *Political Regime*, op. cit. pp. 80-89.
[113]Alfarabi, *Political Regime*, op. cit., pp. 90-95.

material prosperity of its citizens, but also their future destiny. The souls of the citizens of the ignorant state are devoid of reason, and will return to the material elements as sensible forms in order to be united again to other beings, animals or plants.

In both the perverted and mistaken states, the ruler alone is to be held responsible, and he will be punished accordingly in the world hereafter; and the souls which have been led into error share the fate of the citizens of the ignorant state. On the other hand, the good souls will enter the world of pure spirits, and the higher their knowledge in this life, the higher their position after death.[114]

I cannot help quoting the following passage where Alfarabi shows these good souls in possession of their supreme good:

When a great number of men have passed away, and their bodies are annihilated, and their souls made happy, other men will follow them. When these have also passed away and attained the happiness they longed for, each of them joins the one he is similar to in kind and degree. These souls join one another as an intelligible joins an intelligible. In proportion as the souls increase in number and are united to one another, in the same proportion their happiness increases, for, each one, thinking of his substance, thinks of a great many similar substances, and the object of such thinking goes on increasing indefinitely with the arrival of new souls.[115]

The political theory of Alfarabi is a mixture of Platonic and Aristotelian elements. The main Platonic element is to put all humanity in one universal state. For him, the state as it exists now, is not the model state. The model state, not yet realized, is organized humanity which is not circumscribed by national boundaries. It is likened to a family which has in heaven the same Creator and Father, and on earth the same forebears. In such a family there can be no wars, simply because the vision now of each and everyone is not a particular nation, but humanity; not a particular king, but God.

Such a political conception on the part of Alfarabi might surprise the reader, for, we are wont to think that no one could

[114]Alfarabi, *Political Regime*, op. cit. pp. 93-101.
[115]Alfarabi, *Political Regime*, op. cit., pp. 95-96.

# THE PHILOSOPHY OF ALFARABI

ever dream of putting the whole world under one political organization, unless that came as a result of the progress of civilization. But it is not so. Just as the idea of political universality was contained in the imperialism of Alexander the Great, and later in the Roman imperialism, in like manner it was contained in the theocratic Moslem conception. And history bears this out.

Furthermore, Alfarabi tempers the ideal state of Plato with some Aristotelian elements, such as private property and the monarchic form of government. This, however, could be easily changed to an aristocratic republic if the required intellectual and moral traits of the chief executive cannot be found but in a few persons.

In one word, our philosopher envisaged the many nations of the world as welded together into one political organization under a wise ruler.

## CONCLUSION

After studying the philosophy of Alfarabi, one comes to three conclusions; first, that Alfarabi brought about the first penetration of Arabism into Hellenism and of Hellenism into Arabism.

Second, that Alfarabi exerted a great influence on medieval thinkers. This is made clear by the fact that Albertus Magnus quotes Alfarabi, and evidently he could not quote him unless he had known his writings. Hence, the knowledge of the works of Alfarabi gave Albertus Magnus and his pupil, St. Thomas, an opportunity to do some sifting in the sense that they were enabled to throw out the theories that conflicted with Christian teaching and take in at the same time those that appeared to them as logically sound and reconcilable with Christianity.

Third, that Alfarabi improved many Aristotelian theories, solved many problems till then unsolved, and enriched Scholasticism with new philosophical terms, such as quiddity, a necessary being, a contingent being, the speculative and practical intellects, etc.

We have considered the philosophy of Alfarabi under a threefold aspect: the philosophy of being (Metaphysics), the philosophy of thinking (Psychology), and the philosophy of acting (Ethics).

In the philosophy of being, Alfarabi taught that the most universal concept is being, which cannot be defined, nor resolved into simpler concepts. Hence, the simplicity of being of the Latin Schoolmen.

The problem of universals which occupied the minds of medieval thinkers was solved by Alfarabi in the words: "Universale

# THE PHILOSOPHY OF ALFARABI

est unum de multis et in multis." Hence, the traditional definition of the universal, "Aptum praedicari de pluribus."

He also believed that the nature of reality is being in becoming, that is, potentiality and actuality, substance and accident, essence and existence, matter and form, cause and effect. Is all reality that way? Certainly not. For, there is a reality which is beyond all change, and this is God. In comparing the Theodicy of Alfarabi with that of St. Thomas, we found that the latter depends on the former for the first three arguments proving God's existence, and also for the way in which God's nature is known (Via remotionis et eminentiae.)

Furthermore, Alfarabi, three hundred years before St. Thomas, taught in clear and distinct words, that the essence and existence in created things differ as different entities, while they are identical in God. This means that the Saint who came out with the same theory three hundred years later, must certainly have borrowed it from Alfarabi.

In the philosophy of thinking, he describes the history of our speculative intellect. At first it is in potentiality to all things intelligible. It passes from potentiality to act through the action or illumination coming down from above, namely, the active intellect.

In the philosophy of acting, he shows how every human activity tends to happiness. Happiness is the cause that prompts man to live in society, thus creating the state. The model state is the universal state that puts the whole world under one political organization.

In conclusion, there is a unity of thought throughout the philosophy of Alfarabi, who spared no efforts to make the various parts of his philosophical vision converge towards one living God, on Whom the one and the many, being and becoming, are essentially dependent.

# BIBLIOGRAPHY

Dr. T. J. De Boer, *The History of Philosophy in Islam*, English translation by Edward Jones, London, 1903 (Luzac & Co.).

Dr. De Lacy O'Leary, *Arabic Thought and its Place in History*, London, 1922 (Trubner).

*Munk, Melanges de Philosophie Juive Et Arabe*, Paris, 1859 (A. Franck).

A. Schmoelders, *Documenta Philosophiae Arabum* (Bonnae MDCCCXXXVI).

# INDEX

Action, human, 49.
Actuality, 13.
Accident, 13 f.
Appetite, 45 f; sensitive, 45; intellective, 46.
Attribute, divine, 22; not known directly, 22 f.

Being, necessary and contingent, 13; unity and, 13; truth and, 13; goodness and, 13.

Categories, 2 f.
Causality, principle of, 16.
Concept, 1, 10, 40, 41.
Contradiction, principle of, 16.
Contraries, 4 f.

Definition, 1.
Dualism, 32.

Essence, 14; distinct from existence, 14.
Estimative power, 39.
Excluded middle, principle of, 16.
Existence, 14; distinct from essence, 14.

Form, 15.

God, knowability of, 18, 19; proofs of God's existence, 19 f; simplicity of, 23 f; infinity of, 25; immutability of, 25; unity of, 26; intellect of, 27 f; is truth, 28; is life, 28; relation of God to the world, 30.

Imagination, 39.
Intellect, 41, 42; powers of (passive, active, actual, acquired) 42 f.

Judgment, 1.

Knowledge, powers of, 37; sensitive, 38 f; perceptive, 40; abstractive, 41 f.

Logic, 1, 2.

Matter, 15; eternity of, 31 f.
Memory, 39.
Metaphysics, 9; compared with other sciences, 9; division of, 9; general metaphysics, 9; special metaphysics, 9.

Necessity, essential, 4; accidental, 4.

Opposites, 5.

Percept, 40; contrasted with concept, 40, 41.
Potentiality, 13.

Quality, 4.
Quantity, 4.

Relation, 3.

Society, 50.
Soul, 34; spirituality of, 34 f; immortality of, 35 f.
State, model, 50 f; ignorant 51; perverted, 51; mistaken, 51.
Substance, 13; first and second, 10.
Syllogism, 1, 10.

Universal-term, 11; middle term, 1; nature of, 10, 11.